Jun 2, 2008

The *Wild* Water Cycle

by Rena Korb
illustrations by Brandon Reibeling

Content Consultant:
Raymond Hozalski, Ph.D. • Associate Professor of Environmental Engineering • University of Minnesota

visit us at www.abdopublishing.com

Published by Magic Wagon, a division of the ABDO Publishing Group, 8000 West 78th Street, Edina, Minnesota, 55439. Copyright © 2008 by Abdo Consulting Group, Inc. International copyrights reserved in all countries. All rights reserved. No part of this book may be reproduced in any form without written permission from the publisher. Looking Glass Library™ is a trademark and logo of Magic Wagon.

Printed in the United States.

Text by Rena Korb
Illustrations by Brandon Reibeling
Edited by Nadia Higgins
Interior layout and design by Ryan Haugen
Cover design by Brandon Reibeling

Library of Congress Cataloging-in-Publication Data

Korb, Rena B.
 The wild water cycle / Rena Korb ; illustrated by Brandon Reibeling ; content consultant, Raymond Hozalski.
    p. cm. — (Science rocks!)
 ISBN 978-1-60270-041-3
 1. Hydrologic cycle—Juvenile literature. I. Reibeling, Brandon. II. Title.
 GB848.K67 2008
 551.48—dc22
                                    2007006332

Table of Contents

A Rainy Day

Drip. Plop. Splash. It's time to play in the rain!

Hop in a puddle. Twirl your umbrella. Watch a raindrop dangle from the tip of your nose.

Each day about 4 trillion gallons of water fall from the sky. That's enough water to fill 4,000,000,000,000 big milk jugs!

Where did this raindrop come from? Where will it go? How did the rain get in the sky in the first place?

Water All Around

Around and around, the raindrop traveled over Earth. Up and down, it went from the ground into the sky and back again.

Its amazing journey is called the water cycle. Let's follow the rain on its exciting water ride.

The water cycle has been taking place since Earth began. Did you know that water in the raindrop that drips in your eye once dripped in the eye of a dinosaur?

Where Does Rain Go?

Splat! A raindrop hits the ground.
What happens next?

The water may soak the soil. Deep in the
earth, it is stored as groundwater. Slowly,
slowly, the groundwater seeps up into
lakes, rivers, and streams.

11

Watch your step! Rainwater makes small rivers along city streets.

It rushes down drains and into tunnels called storm sewers. The storm sewers may carry the water to a nearby lake or river.

Other raindrops stay above ground. They run downhill until they pour into a creek, stream, river, or lake. Then the raindrops just keep on going.

The water continues flowing down until it mixes into salty oceans.

People can only drink freshwater, not the salty water found in oceans.

15

Deep Oceans

Churning, swirling oceans store almost all the planet's water.

But ocean water does not always stay there. Rays from the hot sun warm the ocean's surface. The heat makes something mysterious happen.

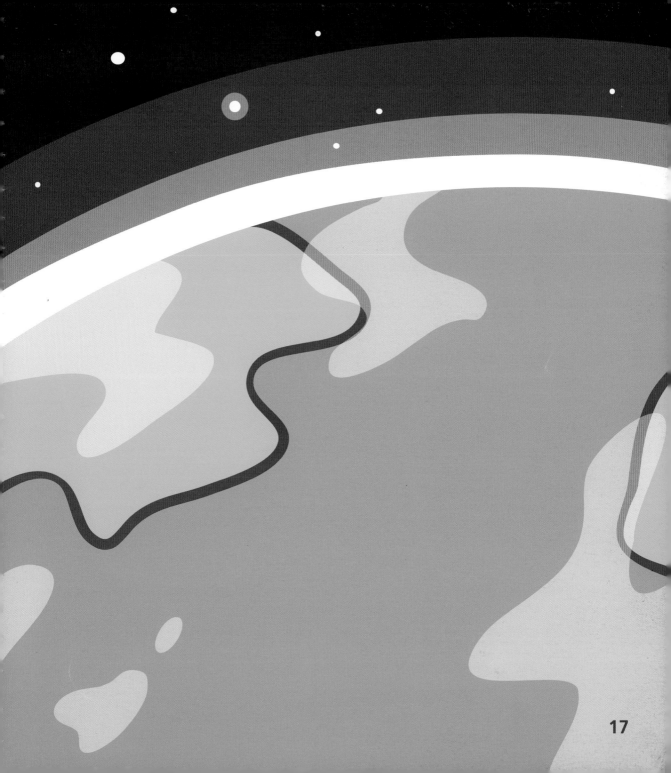

Into the Air

The ocean water changes form! It no longer is a liquid you can spill and splash.
It evaporates. The water becomes part of the invisible air around you.

Day 1

Day 2

This new form of water is called water vapor.
Water vapor rises high into the air.

The air grows colder miles up in the sky.

Clouds Gather

The cold air makes another mysterious thing happen. The water vapor condenses. It changes back into liquid water.

At first, the tiny specs of water are too small to see. But the tiny droplets start gathering together. They form clouds that make shapes in the sky.

What happens when you leave an icy drink out on a hot, muggy day?
The glass gets coated with tiny drops of water.
Water vapor in the air condensed on the cold glass.

The clouds can travel hundreds of miles
while they play and dance high above Earth.

The droplets in the cloud grow heavier
and heavier. The air can no longer hold
them up. The clouds break open.

What if you could put all of the water in a cloud on a scale? You might be surprised to see it weighs as much as a jet airplane!

Rain and Snow

On warm days, rain drizzles or pours from the sky.

In the cold of winter, snow may drift down and blanket the ground.

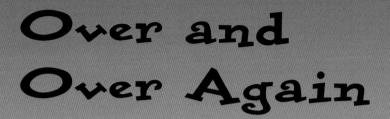

Over and Over Again

Look out your window. Can you see clouds in the sky? Soon raindrops may fall back to Earth. The water cycle will start all over again.

Activity

The Water Cycle in Action

What you need:

A teaspoon

Water

A small plastic bag

A rubber band or twist tie

Tape

A refrigerator

What to do:

1. Place 1 teaspoon of water in the plastic bag.

2. Seal the bag with the rubber band or twist tie. If your bag has a zipper, zip it shut instead.

3. Tape the bag on to a window that gets sunlight.

4. Check the bag several hours later. What changes do you see? What is happening to the water? Remember that heat makes water change form.

5. Now put the bag in the refrigerator.

6. Check the bag several hours later. What changes do you see now? Think about what happens to water vapor when it cools.

Fun Facts

There is 100 times more water underground than there is in all of Earth's lakes and rivers combined.

About two-thirds of the planet's freshwater is frozen in glaciers and ice caps. Greenland, a country in Europe, is almost completely covered in ice.

Rain does not fall in the same amounts around the world. Mount Waialeale in Hawaii gets about 460 inches (1,168 centimeters) of rain each year. That's as high as some four-story buildings. But in Alice Springs, Australia, it only rains about 11 inches (28 centimeters) in one year.

Plants add water vapor to the air. This happens when they lose some water from their leaves.

Earth's oceans formed almost 4 billion years ago. The ocean water probably came from gases escaping from volcanoes. These gases held water vapor. The water vapor rose into the air and formed clouds and rain, just as they still do today.

If you could see Earth from outer space, you'd see mostly white clouds and blue oceans.

Glossary

condense—to change from water vapor into liquid water.

evaporate—to change from liquid water into water vapor.

groundwater—underground supplies of water stored in soil or holes and cracks in rocks.

water cycle—the movement of water from the ground into the sky and back to the ground; the water cycle happens over and over again.

water vapor—water in the form of invisible gas.

On the Web

To learn more about the water cycle, visit ABDO Publishing Company on the World Wide Web at **www.abdopublishing.com**. Web sites about the water cycle are featured on our Book Links page. These links are routinely monitored and updated to provide the most current information available.

Index